For my lovely parents, and in memory of my grandparents who will always have a special place in my heart.

Special thanks to Katie Shmuel and Nicola Marks.

From the author of **Paddy and the Magic Pirate Hat**, **Ben Gives Up His Pacifier**, and **Bea Gives Up Her Pacifier**, winner of a *Prima Baby Award*.

978-0-9934203-2-0   978-0-9934203-1-3   978-0-9926167-5-5

This book belongs to

....

First published in 2014 by Little Boo Publishing
This edition published 2015

ISBN: 978-0-9926167-6-2

From the author of **Bea Gives Up Her Pacifier**.

little boo publishing

Tell Me About Heaven, Grandpa Rabbit!

Written by **Jenny Album**   Illustrated by **Claire Keay**

little boo publishing

Bradley Bunny had a grandpa called 'Grandpa Rabbit'.

Bradley loved
visiting his
grandpa!

Grandpa Rabbit had a wooden box full of fun
games like dominoes. He also had books with
pictures of steam trains, that they would look at together.

Sometimes, when nobody was looking, Grandpa Rabbit would wink at Bradley, and give him candy!

Even when it was nearly time for dinner!

One day, Grandpa Rabbit was getting
ready to go on a big trip around the world.
"Bradley, what gift would you like me
to bring you back from my travels?" he asked.

Bradley thought for a moment.
"I'd like the loveliest seashell
you can find please,
Grandpa," he replied.

Grandpa smiled. "Did you know that if you
put a *special* kind of seashell close to your ear, you
can actually hear the sound of the sea?" he said.

He promised to try and bring Bradley one of those special shells.

When he came back from his trip, Grandpa Rabbit
gave Bradley the biggest seashell he had ever seen.
It was the size of a mango!

It was white and spiky on the outside,
and smooth, shiny and
pink on the inside.

And when Bradley put it to his ear, he could actually *hear* the sound of the sea!

It was soft and *whooshy*, but it was definitely there.

One day, Grandpa Rabbit got sick.
Bradley brought him a big shiny balloon with floppy
arms and a smiley face. Grandpa Rabbit loved it.

He told Bradley that although he had been ill before, this time it was a bit different, and he might be going off to a place called 'Heaven', which was in the sky. He said, "I'll miss everyone when I go, Bradley, but Heaven is a happy place."

"What's Heaven like, Grandpa Rabbit?" asked Bradley.

"Well, Bradley," he replied, "I've always believed
Heaven to be a *super special* place!"

Then Grandpa asked Bradley to imagine a place in the sky,
that felt special to him.

Bradley thought for a moment, then he said, "I imagine a carnival in the sky… But this carnival is especially for bunnies, and it's all about our favorite treat, *carrots*!"

"It has a tall, carrot-shaped slide…

"And a ride with carrot-shaped pods you can sit in.

"There is a 'throw the hoop on the carrot' stand…

"And a stand which sells delicious carroty ice cream and shiny, syrupy candy-carrots on sticks!

"And it has special clouds that bunnies can ride on — made out of fluffy, carrot flavored cotton candy!"

Then, Grandpa Rabbit told Bradley Bunn[y]
how he imagined Heaven to be.

He said, "I think of it as a
beautiful garden in the sky.
On a warm, sunny,
Summer's day.

"There's tasty food sizzling away on a
barbecue…

"And Grandma Rabbecca and Great Aunt Bunnita, (who both went to Heaven a while ago) are there. I'm very excited to see them again!

"We're all talking and laughing together, and having so much fun.

"On the table, there's a plate of hot baked potatoes dripping with butter, and Grandma Rabbecca's delicious chocolate cupcakes, still warm from the oven."

Grandpa Rabbit said that Bradley wouldn't be able to visit him in Heaven, because Heaven was not a place that you could go and visit. But he told him that he would try to keep an eye on him once he got there!

He said "Bradley, if you ever feel sad, you must think of me.
If you do, I'll try to send you a warm hug all the
way from Heaven!"

Bradley went home, and a few days later
Grandpa Rabbit went up to Heaven.

Bradley knew Grandpa Rabbit was happy, and in a special place, so he tried not to feel sad that he had gone.

A few weeks later, Bradley had his friend, Bertie Bunny over to his house to play.

They had great fun together, playing pirates in the garden.

After lunch they played cowboys.

But later on, when they
were playing with Bradley's
trains, Bertie snatched Bradley's
red and blue train away, and
wouldn't let him play with it.

It was Bradley's favorite train.
After that, Bradley didn't
feel much like playing anymore.

After Bertie had gone home, Bradley went up to his bedroom.

He was still feeling a bit sad.

So Bradley decided to do what Grandpa Rabbit had told him he should do, whenever he felt sad.

He thought of Grandpa Rabbit.

Then, the strangest thing happened.
Suddenly, Bradley felt a warm feeling deep inside.

And do you know what? Suddenly, he didn't
feel sad anymore.

Then, Bradley saw the special shell
that Grandpa Rabbit had given him.
He picked it up and put it next to his ear.

And guess what?
He could *hear*
the sound
of the sea.

It was soft and *whooshy*, but it was definitely there.

CPSIA information can be obtained
at www.ICGtesting.com
Printed in the USA
BVHW02s1810160518
516406BV00025B/415/P